Creepy Crawly ABC

lambkinz

Watch this book come to life in the **lambkinz** app

where books come to life

Download now on

or watch exclusively on
watch.lambkinz.com

A

ant

bumblebee

B

C cockroach

D

dragonfly

E e

earthworm

F firefly

G

grasshopper

hummingbird moth

H

 inchworm

J

june bug

katydid

L

Ladybug

M

mosquito

netwing

O owlfly

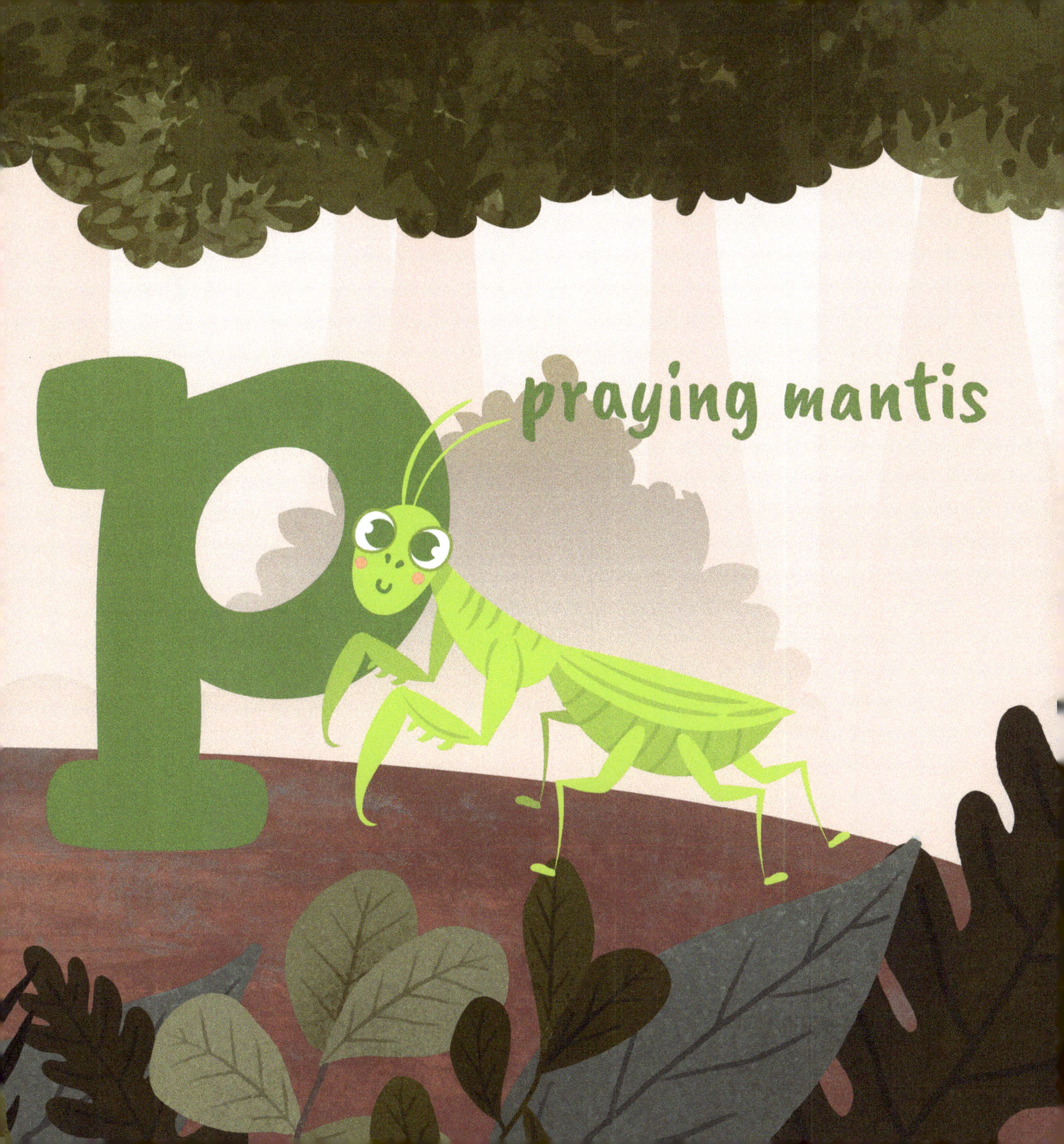
p
praying mantis

queen bee

rhino beetle

S

snail

T

three-lined
potato beetle

U underwing

V velvet ant

walking stick

W

xerces

yellow harlequin bug

zebra butterfly

Z

Explore more titles

ننھی ہیرو
کریم ارفع
مرتب کردہ: لیکیلیز

بقرعید
مبارک
تحریر صوفیہ ناصر

حضرت یوسف
اور بادشاہ کا خواب

حضرت یونس
اور مچھلی

پیاری باتیں
دو ابم الفاظ
تحریر
ناصر حسین

پیاری باتیں
پڑھنا
اچھا لگتا ہے
تحریر
ناصر حسین

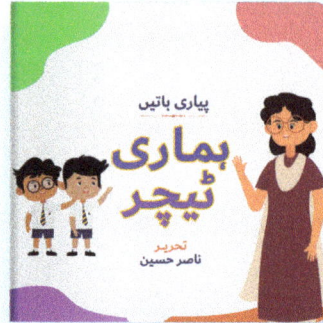

پیاری باتیں
ہماری ٹیچر
تحریر
ناصر حسین

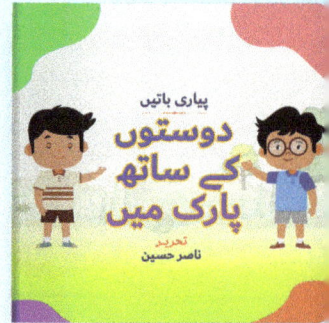

پیاری باتیں
دوستوں
کے ساتھ
پارک میں
تحریر
ناصر حسین

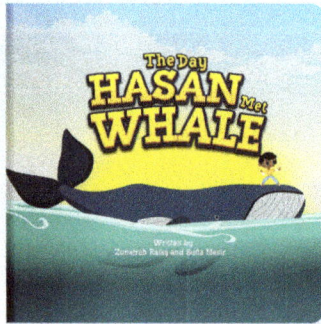

The Day
HASAN Met
WHALE
Written by
Zumeruh Raiss and Safia Meer

سدرہ کی بلی
تحریر
صوفیہ ناصر

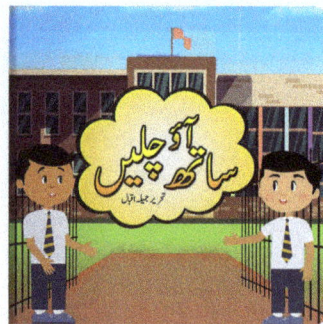

آؤ چلیں
ساتھ
تحریر جلد اول

قومی ترانے
کی عظمت

Watch all our books come to life with playful animation, gentle music & lifelike sound effects in the lambkinz app

lambkinz
where books come to life

lambkinz combines the joy of reading storybooks with playful animation. lambkinz features dozens of gorgeous original stories, general knowledge & instructionals for kids to enjoy & learn from.

Download the **lambkinz** app for your device.

Download on the **App Store**

GET IT ON **Google Play**

lambkinz is a registered trademark of Green Animation Studio

www.ingramcontent.com/pod-product-compliance
Lightning Source LLC
Chambersburg PA
CBHW060754150426
42811CB00058B/1400